Brainstorming for Problems Solving

How Leaders Can Achieve a Successful Brainstorming Session

I0481007

While every precaution has been taken
in the preparation of this book, the
publisher assumes no responsibility for
errors or omissions, or for damages
resulting from the use of the
information contained herein.

BRAINSTORMING FOR PROBLEM
SOLVING: HOW LEADERS CAN
ACHIEVE A SUCCESFFUL
BRAINSTORMING SESSION

First edition. October 11, 2020.

**Written by: Mohammed Hamed Ahmed
Soliman**

Contents

Dedication

I created this book with the help of more than fifteen different business resources. These academic articles and books are all cited at the end of this book. A number of people have influenced my learning journey and my entire career. I would like to acknowledge them here.

Esraa Soliman: My lovely wife and partner. She encouraged me to write and publish this work. In fact, she always encourages me to do creative work.

Jeffrey Liker: Professor at the University of Michigan and author of *The Toyota Way* and the amazing Toyota series of books. His impressive work on Toyota inspired and influenced my learning about the Toyota Production System. I would really like to thank him for his indirect involvement in this work. Many examples included in this book were originally from his books. Although I have never met Jeff face to face, we have had great communications over social media platforms.

Chris Duklet: A lean manufacturing leader from the United States who works in the field of health care. He has contributed to this work by reviewing the book prior to publication and giving me useful recommendations and advice.

Attia Gomaa: Professor at the American University in Cairo who influenced my teaching career at the university and taught me how to become a good trainer.

Steven Borris: A business consultant, author, and friend from England who influenced my writing career. He encouraged me to write and publish. Steven was my mentor on lean manufacturing, helping me first to understand the basics, after which I developed my understanding through deep practice and self-directed learning.

Eslam Soliman: My friend and a professor at the Assiut University. His PhD is from the University of New Mexico. He has influenced my entire writing career by giving me recommendations and advice on how to write and publish. He revised my published works many times and kept inspiring me after every piece I wrote and published.

What is Brainstorming?

A quality tool for issues comprehending that ought to be a contributor to any issues tackling practice.

Brainstorming is a conceptualizing technique that is a notable strategy for creating countless thoughts in a brief timeframe period. It fills in as an instrument for recognizing issues and causes.

To energize thoughts, no thought ought to be scrutinized or remarked when advertised. Every thought ought to be recorded and numbered, precisely as offered on a flip outline.

Hope to produce in any event 50 to 60 thoughts in a 30 minutes meeting to generate new ideas.

> Brainstorming helps to collect the data needed for any Total Quality Management Process

Brainstorming Rules

T• ry not to remark on, judge or evaluate thoughts as advertised.
• Support inventive and odd thoughts.

- An enormous number of thoughts is the objective.
- Assess thoughts later.

> When the brainstorming session is over, the ideas should be reviewed, similar ideas combined, and ideas that do not seem to fit eliminated.

Brainstorming is a group problem-solving method. It taps people creative ability to identify and solve problems, and brings out a lot of ideas in a very short time. Because it is a group process, it helps builds people as human beings. For example, brainstorming encourages individual members to contribute to the group and to develop trust for the other members.

What is Required for Brainstorming?

A **gathering ready to cooperate**
You may feel it is unthinkable that the gathering you work with will never be a group. Be that as it may, conceptualizing can be a key to manufacture a group! Besides, it is an incredible apparatus for the gathering which is as of now cooperating.

Who ought to be remembered for the gathering?

Each and every individual who is worried for the issue for two reasons: the thoughts for every individual who worried about the difficult will be accessible for the talk. Second, those individuals can take a functioning part in tackling the issue. In that manner they can be got the chance to help the arrangement.

1. A pioneer
- The principal parts of the pioneer are:
- Give some direction so conceptualize will deliver thoughts
- Authority over the gathering to keep them on target.
- Empower individuals' thoughts and interest.
- Set the individual objectives aside to help the gathering.

2. A gathering place
A spot where there is no interference or interruption. In certain plants, bunches utilize a foreman office, a region on the creation floor, or even a meeting room.

3. Resources or Tools
Flipcharts, markers, and white sheets

How Does it Work?

- ✓ Pick a subject for the talk.
- ✓ Ensure that everybody comprehend what the issue or the subject is.
- ✓ Every individual is to take a turn an express one thought. On the off chance that somebody can't consider anything, the individual in question says "pass". In the event that somebody thinks about a thought when it isn't his turn, he may wright it down on a paper and use it at his next turn.
- ✓ Record every thought precisely as communicated.
- ✓ Try to compose all thoughts and don't dismiss any.
- ✓ Energize wild thoughts, they may trigger another person's reasoning.
- ✓ Hold criticism until after the session.
- ✓ The main goal is quantity and creativity.

- ✓ A little laughter is fun and healthy but don't overdo. It is O.K to laugh with someone but not at them.
- ✓ Allow few hours or days for further thoughts (if needed). The first brainstorm on a subject will stimulate people to start thinking, but an incubation period allow mind to release more creative ideas and thoughts.

Example: Conducting a Brainstorming Session
Conceptualizing the Causes of a Defective Capacitor

This gathering incorporates five individuals: Samy, the pioneer; Farouk; Mohammed; Gamal, the recorder, and Ahmed. Since they have been meeting for just a brief timeframe and the individuals have not had a lot of involvement in conceptualizing, the pioneer needs to do a large portion of crafted by keeping them on target. As the gathering picks up experience, different individuals should start to share crafted by the initiative.

Samy: I believe it's an ideal opportunity to conceptualize for reasons for flawed capacitors. Gamal, since you are acceptable at flip outline, would you be able to help us there?

Gamal: Yes obviously.

Samy: Let us set a 15 minutes time cap for the meeting. What's more, remember the standards: We will go around from individual to another, one thought at time. Try not to stress if your thought sound unusual. All things considered, regardless of whether your thought is a wild one, it might invigorate another person. No assessments. We will have a lot of time thereafter to take a gander at the thoughts. Alright would you say you are prepared? (Everyone concurs.)

Farouk, your turn.

Farouk: Vendor (Gamal records, VENDOR).

Mohammed: I have seen gouges in some of them. Furthermore, I feel that a mark outwardly implies something breaks or gets pressed or somehow wrecked inside.

Samy: Mohammed, you are stating "gouges". Is that right?

Mohammed: No, I mean gouges show us there is an issue inside.

Samy: Can we abridge it to peruse: "Imprints show inside issue"?

(Mohammed gestures "O. K"

Samy: Gamal, it's your turn.

Gamal: I figure I will relax.

Ahmed: The prompts the capacitor now and then doesn't get fastened well. So, makes it resemble a blemished capacitor.

Gamal: How would I compose that? "Binding of leads"?

Ahmed: Yup that is O.K.

Samy: My turn. I will expand on Farouk's concept of "seller". May be its just one of them that is actually the issue and not every one of them. Gamal state "One Vendor"

Farouk: Seems to me the state of AX12's is the issue. They help me to remember the latrine seats spread. (Much Laughter).

Samy: Let's return to the subject. Farouk, may have something there. So Samy express "State of AX12's".

Tips and Techniques for Completing the Session

Nudging Techniques
Also called "prodding' technique. Sooner or later the downpours of ideas in the brainstorm dries up. What do you do to get it going again? Or what do you do with the silent member who doesn't participate?

Empowering Thoughts: making preparations once more "priming the pump again"
If the brainstorming session seems to slow down, the leader may suggest piggybacking. Piggybacking is building on others' ideas. For example, if one of the team members has suggested the vendor as a cause of the problem, another one might say "one vendor" not all of them could be the reason of the problem.

Another technique is to suggest opposites. For example, too much & too little.

Dealing with the silent member

When a member of the group doesn't speak up, the best way to deal with this is to be patient.

Sometimes a person will be quiet for a meeting after meeting then he will open up. It will be then very exciting, so give this person a time. Maybe he/she will be quiet, but will serve the group with some other ways.

A simple effective method to bring the silent member, is to remind the whole group that when each person's turn comes in the brainstorm, he or she just says "Pass" if not ready with an idea. That gets people of the hock but it also breaks the sound barrier. They hear their own voices and participate by saying "Pass."

The direct question is another method, but you must use it with care.

Something like" Mohammed, you know the process well, do you have a suggestion or input here?"

The Second Session

After the initial brainstorm and sometime for further thinking, it's a good idea to have another session to capture more ideas. These ideas come into mind as the group member think about the problem and consider what was said in the first session.

Two different ways to deal with the subsequent meeting:

Assemble all gathering and give them a period cutoff of 10-12 minutes for extra thoughts. Similar principles applied as in the primary meeting.

Post the conceptualizing sheets in the territory of the working environment with the goal that it will permit individuals who work in a similar region to contribute regardless of whether they are not a normal individual from the critical thinking gathering. In that manner they believe they are not forgotten about.

Finishing a talk

How would you ensure that conceptualizing has secured all potential reasons for an issue?

Here and there the arrangement lies in a pursuit lab, where just a high prepared master gets an opportunity of uncovering it. Frequently, in this way, the arrangements are directly close to home.

Regardless of whether you don't tackle the issue immediately, you can ensure that you have secured all the overall zones of potential causes. Make a rundown of the overall regions, and ensure that you're gathering or group has analyzed all of them.

Such a list would include a number of subjects. There are some major factors that go into an operation: management, machine, method, material, environment, and people.

Machine include: the type of the machine, the maintenance, and the setting.

Materials are the elements that come to the process, whether they are raw material, sub-assemblies, components, or partially processed materials.

Method concerns the process itself.

Environment is important too, humidity, dust, and other climate problems that may affect the process.

Management concerning procedures standards, training and leadership.

Finally, the Person doing the job. Factors connected with the person could be training, eyesight, and level of skills.

Other general areas may also apply to the problem. Such as money, process, and other errors.

Troubles and How to Manage Them
You are stepping on my turf!

I t will be hard for one of the gathering individuals to be associated that he is the reasons with this issue. For instance, the plan engineer is going to the meeting, and the reason for the issue came out to be in the plan cycle.

Train your group, and create them. It is important to clarify that we are not here to accuse anybody. What's more, we are at times dazzle with our issues so we need others to look on it. We will in general observe just a contributor to the issue that is the reason the causes might be covered up. It involves forthcoming.

Analysis
Fabricate a positive climate in the gathering. Censure issues not individuals. Ensure that thoughts not people are assessed. Ensure that errors are not announced and never show up in anybody individual life.

The troublesome part

A few individuals are hard to manage in the gathering. They blabber, they get off track, they scrutinize individuals not thoughts or they destroy thoughts. How would you manage him?

Be firm however cordial. Converse with him secretly and clarify how his way is diverting the gathering work. Give the troublesome part an uncommon employment to accomplish for the gathering. Try not to battle him. At the point when he gets the gathering off course, re back the discussion to the ordinary theme tenderly.

Generally troublesome individuals turned into the most grounded help of the gathering, or they leave.

Appendix. I: Fault-Tree Analysis

I s a method to increase the reliability of the product and find the potential causes of a problem to prevent the product failure. The method uses inputs from brainstorming sessions.

Building a fault tree analysis FTA:
1) Identify a top failure
2) Brainstorm basic contributors to failure
3) Link contributors to the top failure
Determine which combination of contributors is needed to cause the top failure. (Ask: How many of the inputs are needed to cause the top failure?)
Link the contributors to the top failure. Each contributor (cause) can be given a weight depend on the occurrence so we would know which failure is likelihood to occur.

Fault-Tree Analysis

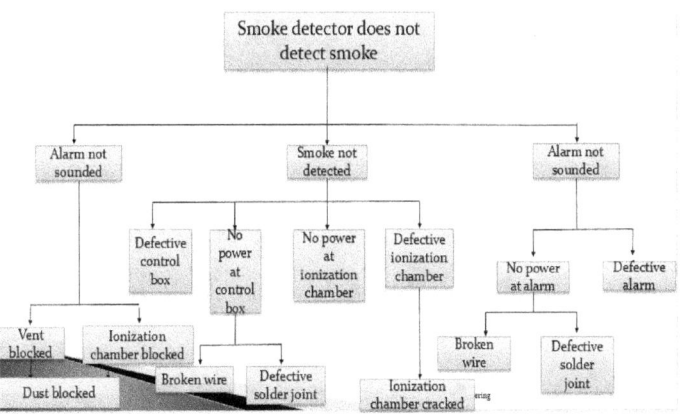

Appendix. II: Cause and Effect Diagram 5 Whys

5 whys are the method of completing the cause-and-effect diagram to tackle the root cause of the problem and prevent recurrent failure. It was originated in Japan. Japanese people believe that by asking 5 whys you can figure out the root cause of the problem and find the solution. However, it doesn't have to be 5 it can be 7 or 8.

Toyota

Toyota does not have a six-sigma program. Six sigma is based on complex statistical quality analysis tools. It is a surprise for people to realize how Toyota has achieved this level of quality without the use of six sigma for quality.

Most of problems don't call for complex statistical analysis, but instead require detailed problem solving. This requires a level of detailed thinking and analysis that is all too absent from most companies in day-

to-day activities.

Level of Problem	Countermeasure
There is an oil on the shop floor	Clean up the oil
Because the machine is leaking	Fix the machine
Because the gasket has deteriorated	Replace the gasket
Because we bought gaskets made of inferior material	Change gasket specifications
Because we got a good deal/price on those gaskets	Change purchasing policy
Because the purchasing gets evaluated on short-term cost saving	Change the evaluation policy for purchasing agent

Why?
Why?
Why?
Why?

5 whys is a method to pursue the deeper, systematic causes of a
problem to find correspondingly deeper countermeasures

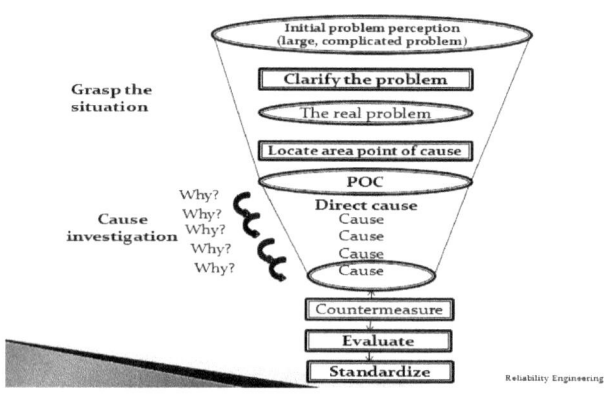

Toyota Practical Problem-Solving Process

Reliability Engineering

Example:

Q1: Why did the customer not buy the product?

A: The salesperson did not persuade him to buy.

Q2: Why did the salesperson not persuade the customer to buy?

A: The salesperson was not good enough.

Q3: Why was the salesperson not good enough?

A: The sales person has not been trained in sales.

Q4: Why has the salesperson not been trained in sales?

A: It was not considered necessary.

Q5: Why was training not considered necessary?

A: Sales are only a small part of the job.

Drawing Cause and Effect Diagram (Fishbone Diagram)

Using a fishbone diagram while brainstorming possible causes helps you to focus on the various possibilities. Some useful categories:

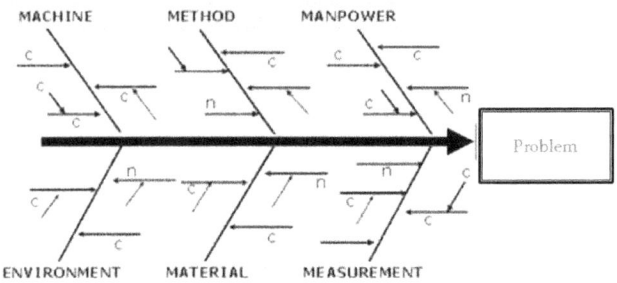

The main problem is entered in the nose. The bones originally had only "4Ms". Once all problems were reduced to one of the four: man, machine, material, or method. Eventually, **measurement** was added to highlight how critical it is to have an understanding of the reliability and accuracy of the measuring system. **Environment** was added to make people consider the location of an equipment and the impact of its surroundings on the operation. **Design** and instruction can also be a good reason to add.

Fishbone diagram take inputs from brainstorming sessions. Those possible countermeasures are the ideas that people give during the brainstorming sessions. Dig deep into the details at the Gemba (the place where real work happens) is necessary to absorb the real situation, perform diagnosis, make analysis, talk to people that are involved directly in the work and base the solution on facts.

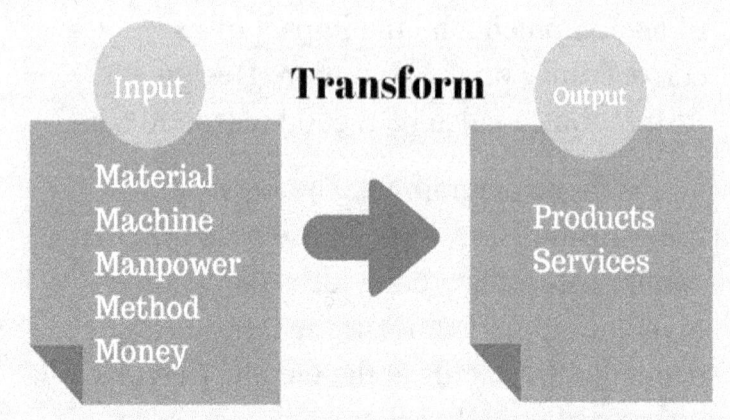

Steps in constructing a cause-and-effect diagram

1. Gather the material

You will need a big flip chart or large sheet of paper, brainstorm idea list, mistake tape and flipchart markers.

2. Call together everyone involved with the problem

Generally, this group will contain the leader and the members of the brainstorm group. Plus, anyone involved such as engineers, representatives, quality assurance peoples and a volunteer to draw the diagram and record the data.

3. Begin to construct the diagram

Got to the right-hand side, and state the problem clearly or the effect. Make sure it is well defined and clear so everyone will understand what is going to be discussed.

4. Draw in the spine of the fish bone

Begin with the left hand of the paper and
draw an arrow to the box

Variation in Coating

Machine, Material). Also add up some other
sections like environment such as humidity,
high temperature. etc.

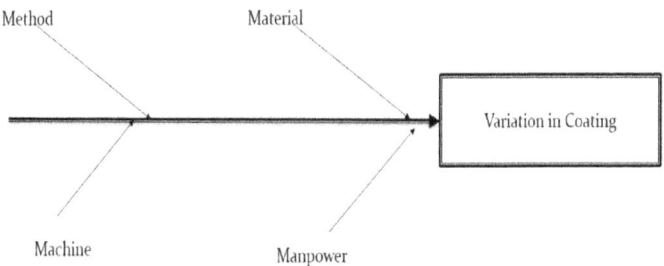

6. Add the brainstorm ideas

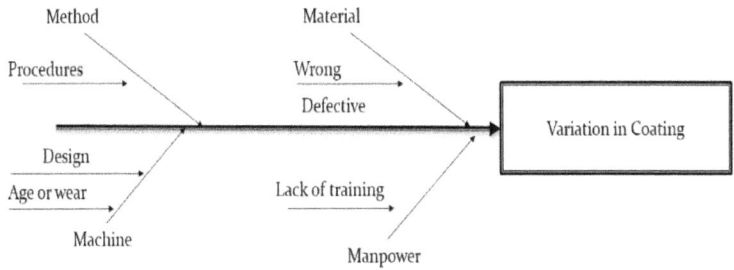

APPENDIX.III: PARETO ANALYSIS

What is Pareto analysis?
A method to help you which from several chronic problems to attack. Pareto can be useful in:

1. Prioritizing issues and tasks.

2. Tackle high-cost issues.

3. Achieve quick improvement in the overall process.

4. Help making decisions.

5. Help determine whether the solution has worked.

Few examples:

- 20% percent of your customers account for 80% of your business.

- Few kinds of parts in the warehouses make 80% of the inventory problems.

- Few parts present a large portion of product defect.

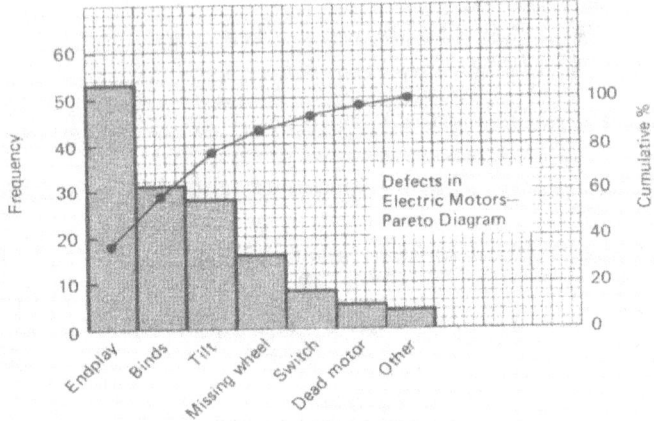

A team collected a data about a defect in motors produced by their department. Among the 145 defects recorded, they found 53 causes of Endplay, 31 causes of Binds, 28 Causes of Tilt, 16 Missing Wheels, 8 Switch problems, 5 Dead motors.

A Case of Tackling Defects

T ackling Defects in Manufacturing the Polyurethane Foam Cushions.

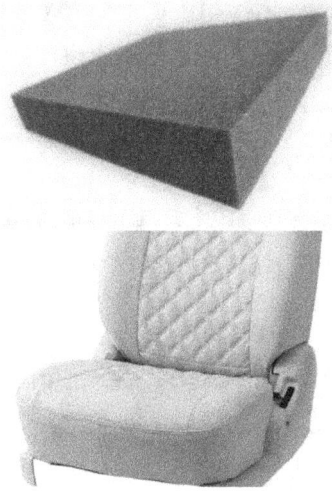

Practical Steps: How to construct a Pareto analysis process

1. Specify the goal clearly

Goals are always improving quality and reducing costs. If your company supplies seats to a major automotive industry firm, the goal should be supplying seats with the highest quality.

Your department makes the polyurethane foam cushions that goes into the seats.

Your goal is to improve the quality of the seats through improving the quality of the cushions, and reduce the rate of the defective cushions.

The Goal is Zero Defect!

2. Collecting the data

Audit Inspection Report		Shift:			
Auditor Name:		Product:			
Departement: Molding		Date: August 2005			
Type of Defect	**12/8**	**13/8**	**14/8**	**15/8**	**16/8**
Poor mix	2		3	1	
Holes	8	4	7	3	5
Dent		1			
No enough component	1		1		
Deformed					1
Torn through handling	1				
Oil/grease stains		1	1	1	1

3. Tally the data

Tally of Data	
Poor mix	6
Holes	27
Dent	1
No enough component	2
Deformed	1
Torn through handling	1
Oil/grease stains	2
Poor mix	3
Total Defects = 42	

4. Ranking the categories of defects by frequency

Re arrange in order of frequency	
Holes	27
Poor mix	6
Oil/grease stains	3
Not enough components	2
Torn through handling	2
Dents	1
Deformed	1
Total Defects = 42	

5. Prepare the chart for the data

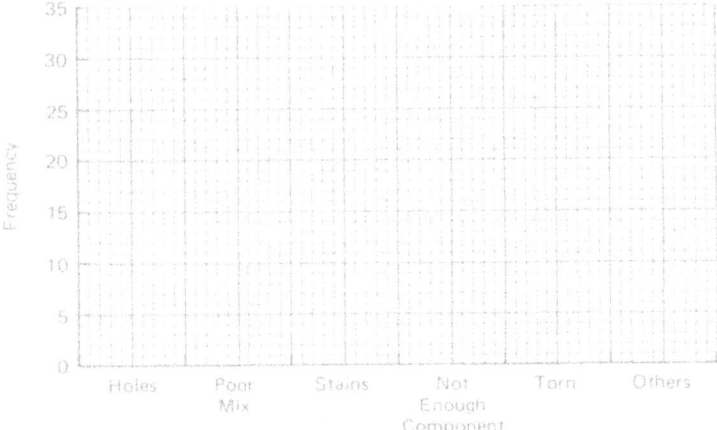

Draw horizontal and vertical scales. Then mark the numbers on the left-hand vertical scale so that the large category will fit comfortably. The largest category is holes with 27 defects, the scale should be set to 35 or 40.

Next, subdivide the horizontal scale into equal width interval so that you have enough intervals for your categories. You can combine the smallest categories into a single group called "others" but it is recommended

that this group should not exceed 10% of the
total numbers.

6. Draw in the bars

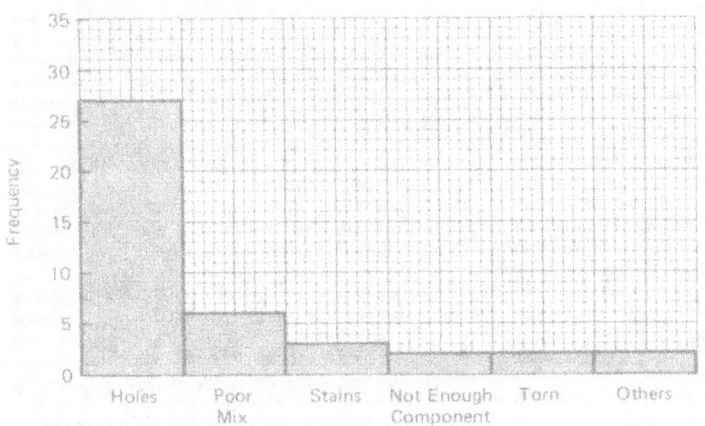

7. Make Calculations Based on Tallies

Type of Defect	Frequency	Cumulative	
		Frequency	Percentage
Holes	27	27	64%
Poor mix	6	33	79%
Oil/grease stains	3	36	86%
Not enough components	2	38	90%
Torn through handling	2	40	95%
Others	2	42	100%

8. Complete the Pareto diagram

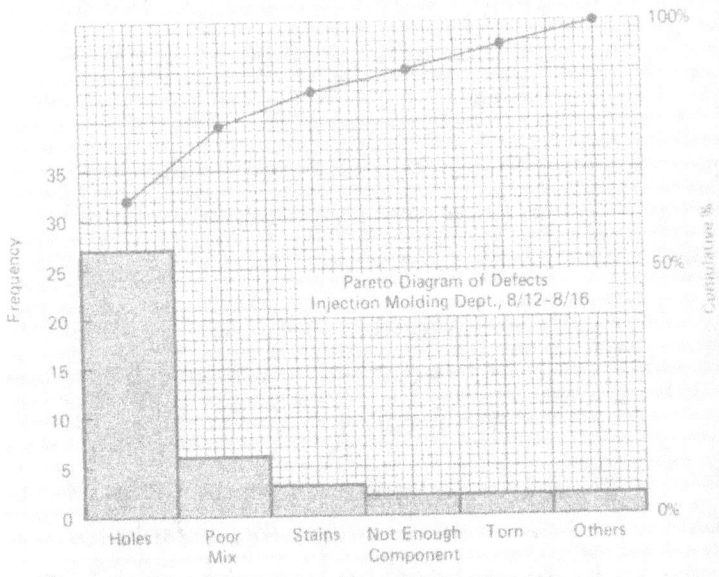

Pareto Diagram of Defects
Injection Molding Dept., 8/12–8/16

Interpreting the Pareto diagram

- The diagram is a documentation for quality, so it has to be clear and well-drawn.

- The diagram is a communication tool, and it brings agreement on which problem to solve first.

- The diagram should allow the process to tell its own story without the human feeling.

- Pareto diagram serves as a way to compare problems that exist before you work to improve the process with problems that exist after you have worked on the process.

- After the "holes" problem is tackled, a new Pareto chart should show holes as a minor or nonexistent problem.

Case Study: Plant Productivity Analysis

Plant Capacity: 450ton/day.
Problem Identification: Production decreased to low level.

Production history for the past 9 months.

Monthly Average Production per day

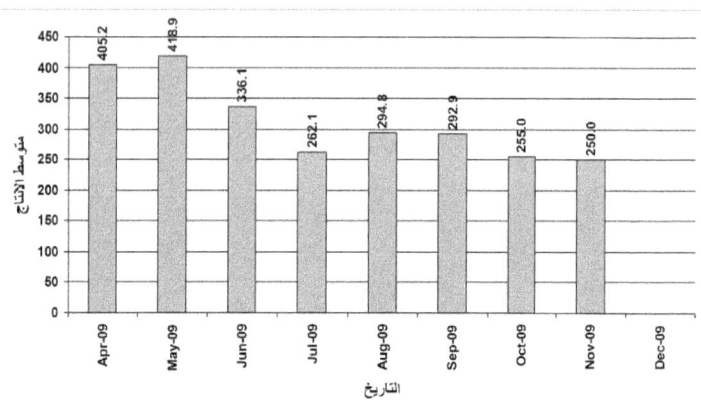

Investigate Why

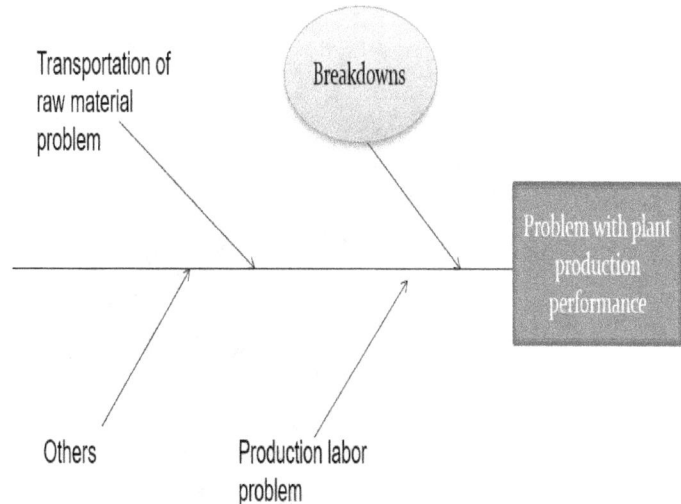

Investigate Why

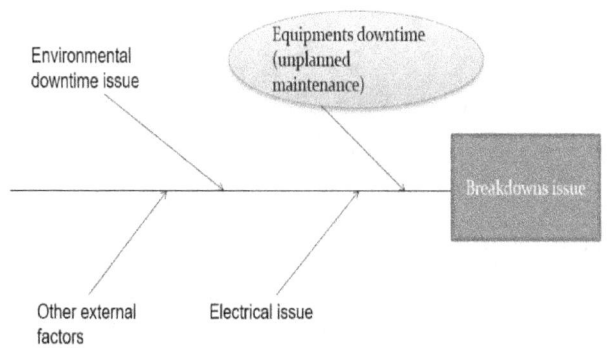

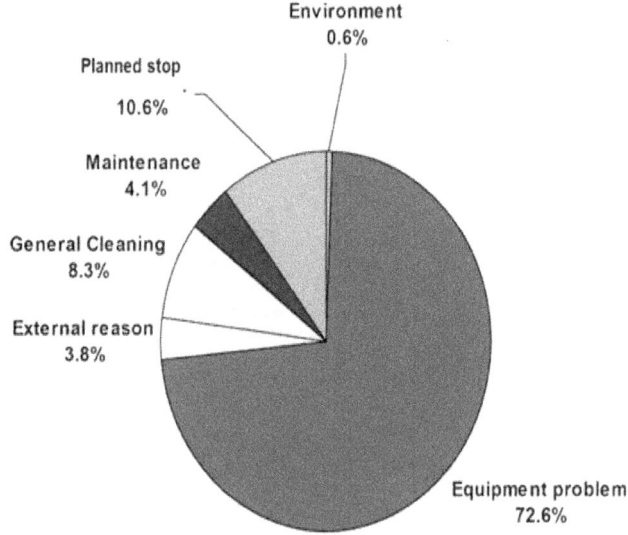

Investigate Why

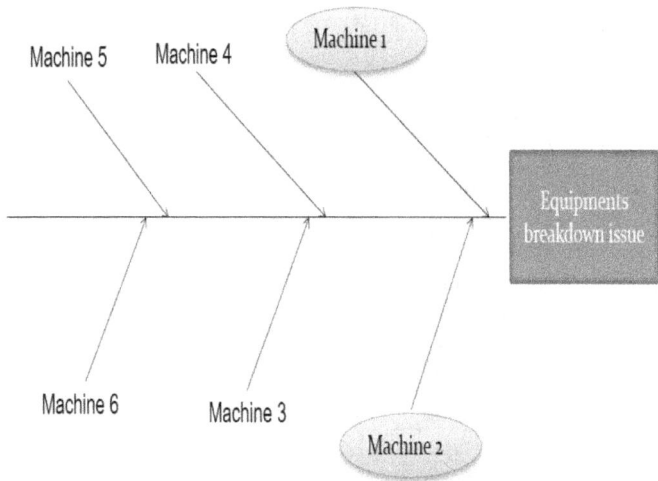

Priority Identification (Top Failures)

Equipment downtime monthly report:

Equip code	Critical Equip description	Total Downtime hrs (average)	Downtime frequency	MTTR (hrs)	Percentage
1	Centrifugal Fan	16	5	3.2	44.80%
2	Pump station 2 Motor	6	2	3	16.80%
3	Granulator Drum	4	2	2	11%
4	Feed Belt Conveyor	3	2	1.5	8.40%
5	Recycle Belt Conveyor	2.5	1	2.5	7.00%
6	Bag Filter	2.5	1	2.5	7%
7	Burner	1	1	1	2%
8	Belt Conveyor	0.5	1	0.5	1.40%
9	Belt Conveyor	0.2	1	0.2	1.40%
10	Bucket Elevator	----	----	----	----

Pareto Analysis☐ A problem solving tool that breaks data down into manageable groups and identifies the greatest opportunity for return on investment. The analysis is based on the Pareto Principle, also known as the 80:20 Rule. Simply stated, the principle says that 20% of a population will cause 80% of the problems associated with the population

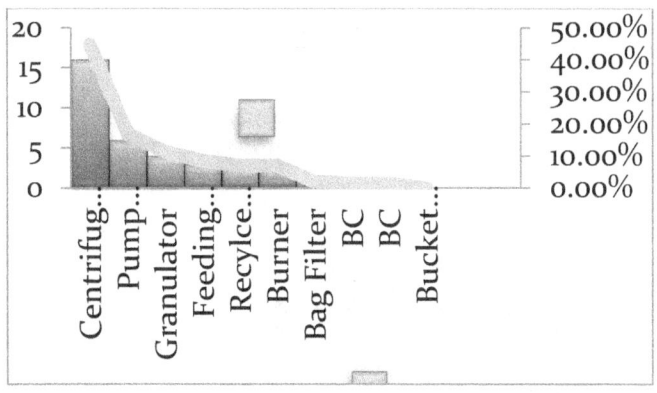

Pareto diagram uses bar graphs to sort problems according to severity, frequency, cost, nature, or source and displays them in order of size in order of size to show which problem is the most important. It's probably the most often used statistical tool in Toyota.

<u>Centrifugal Fan (Machine1)</u>

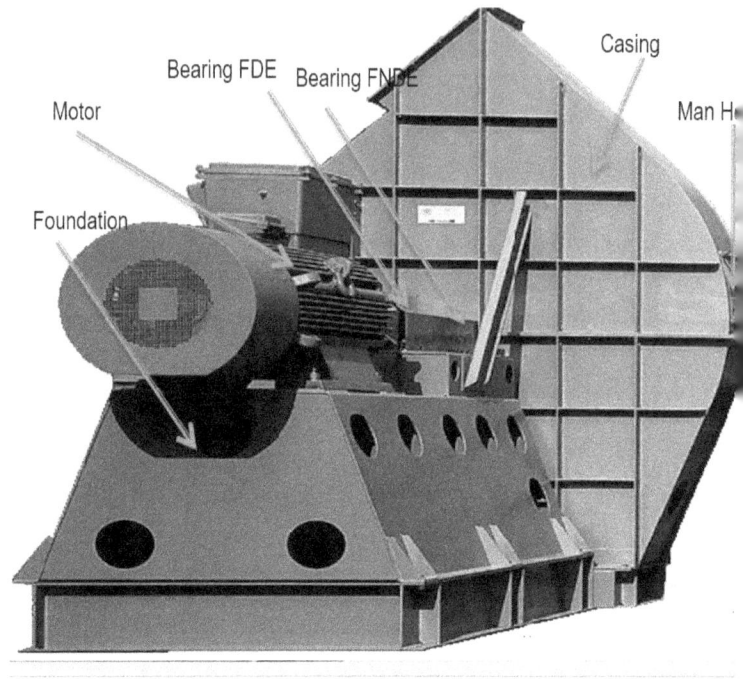

Investigate Why

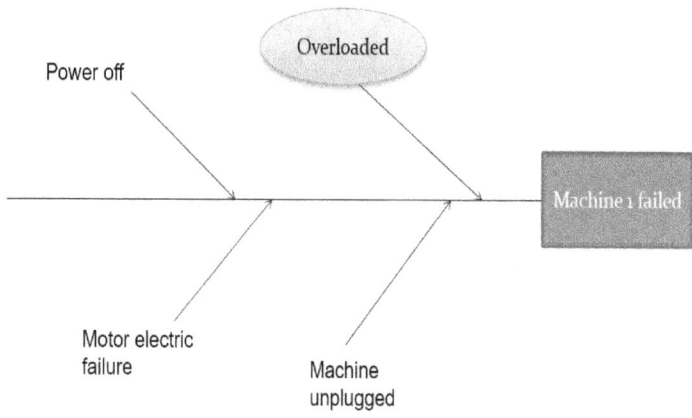

Investigate Why

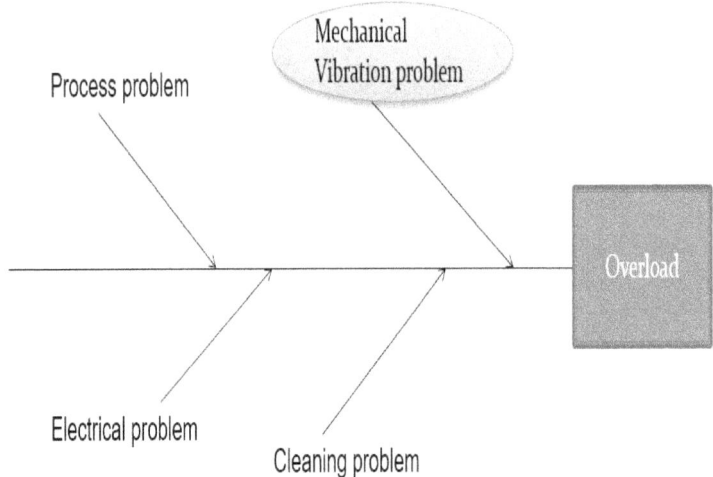

Investigate Why

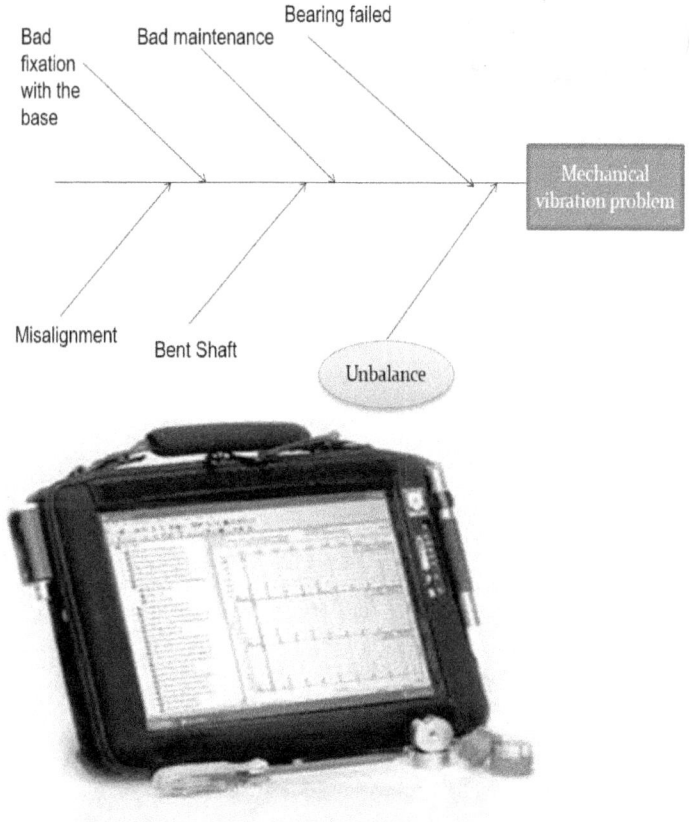

Vibration Analyzer

Investigate Why

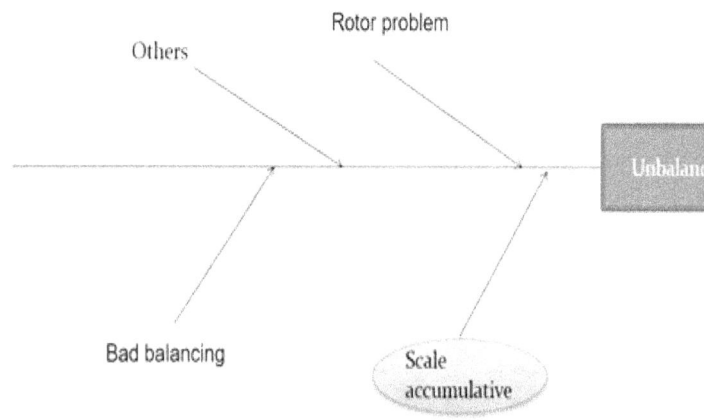

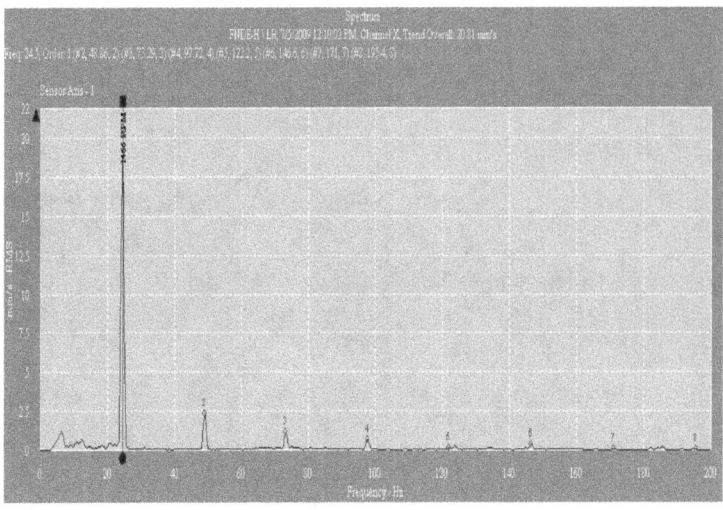

Investigate Why

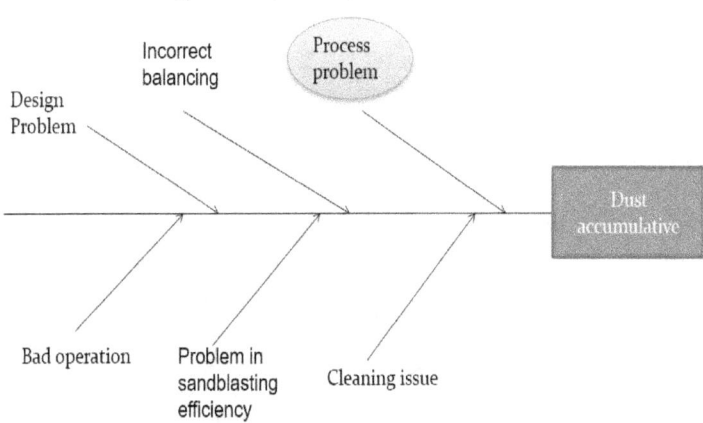

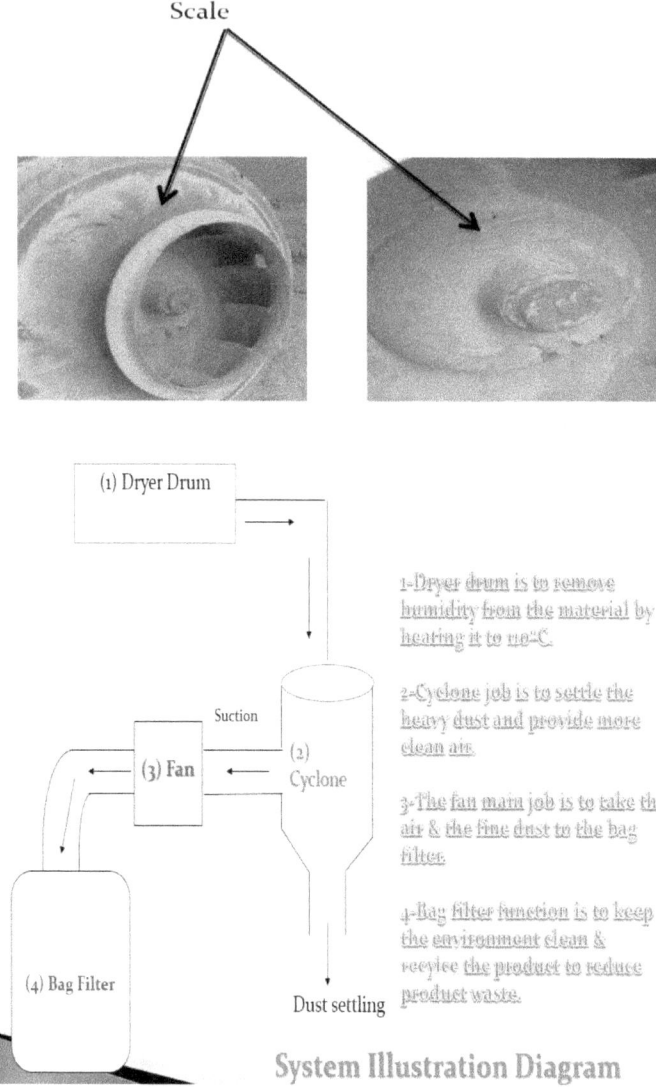

Scale

(1) Dryer Drum

Suction

(3) Fan

(2) Cyclone

(4) Bag Filter

Dust settling

1-Dryer drum is to remove humidity from the material by heating it to 110°C.

2-Cyclone job is to settle the heavy dust and provide more clean air.

3-The fan main job is to take the air & the fine dust to the bag filter.

4-Bag filter function is to keep the environment clean & recycle the product to reduce product waste.

System Illustration Diagram

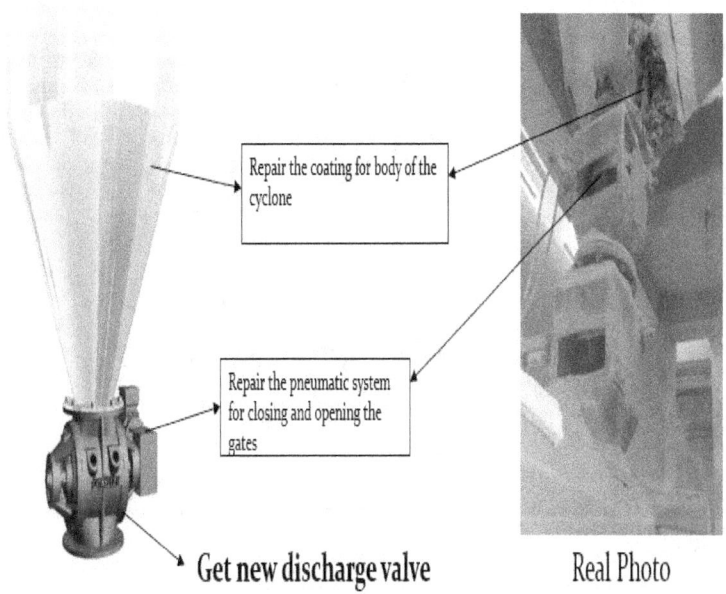

Repair the coating for body of the cyclone

Repair the pneumatic system for closing and opening the gates

Get new discharge valve

Real Photo

Machine.2 Motor

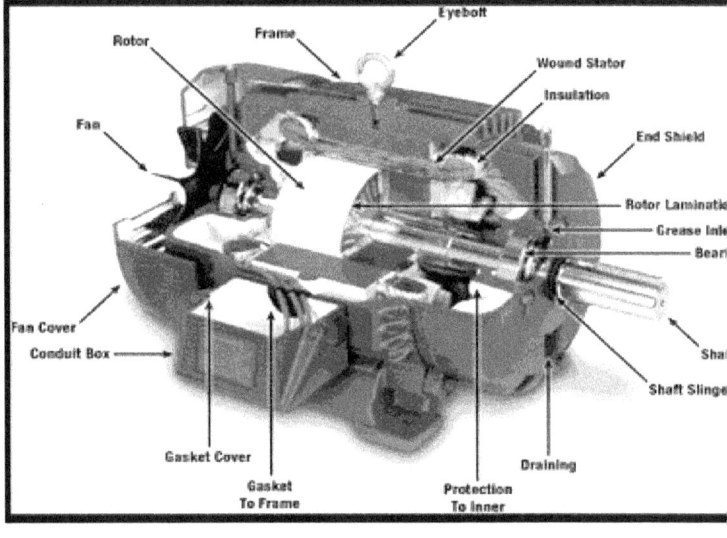

Investigate Why

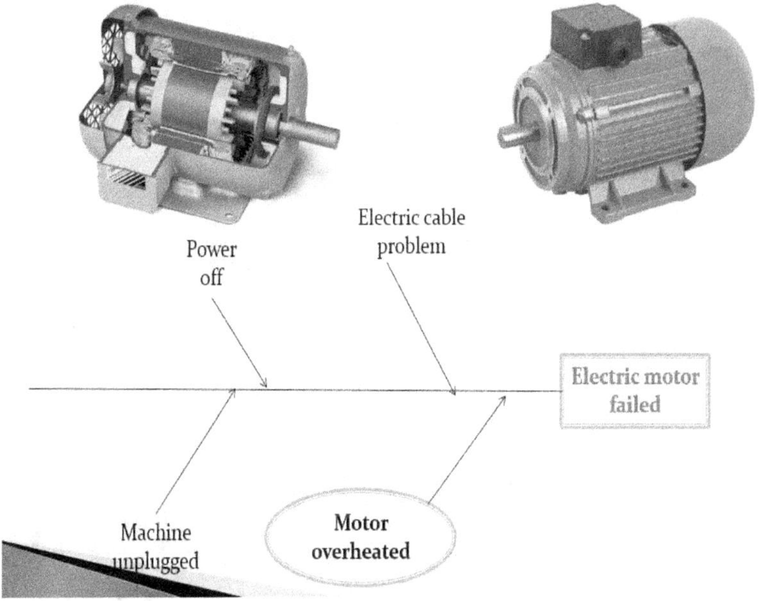

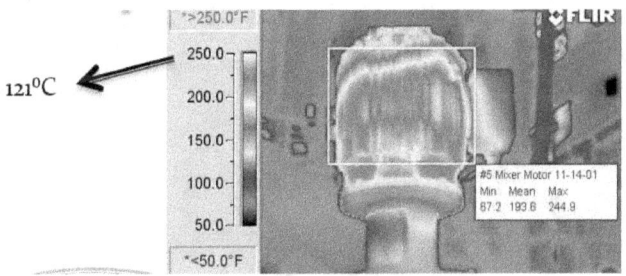

Power off
Electric cable problem
Electric motor failed
Machine unplugged
Motor overheated

Investigate Why

121°C
*>250.0°F
250.0
200.0
150.0
100.0
50.0
*<50.0°F
FLIR
#5 Mixer Motor 11-14-01
Min Mean Max
87.2 193.6 244.9

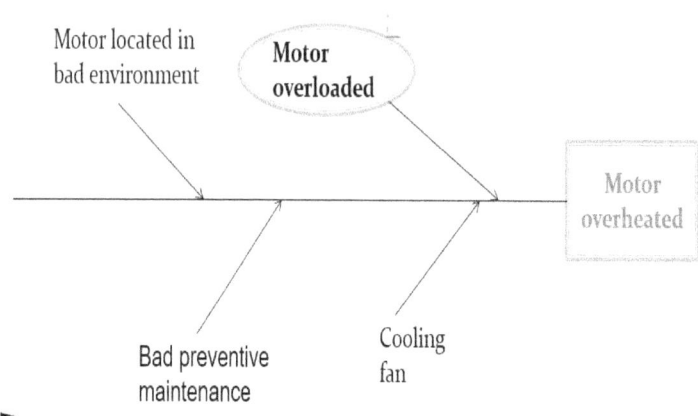

Investigate Why

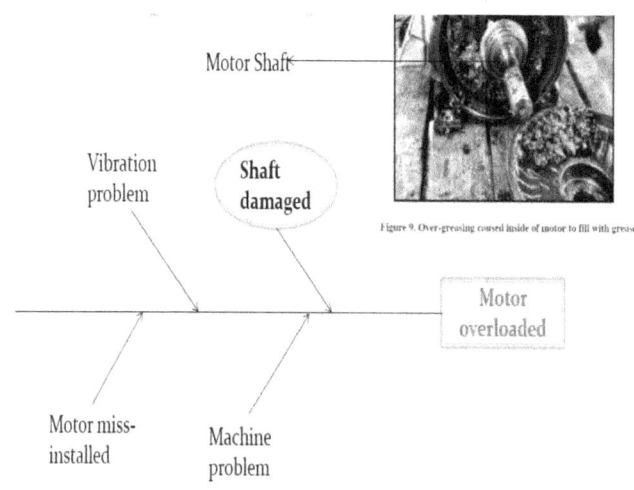

Figure 9. Over-greasing caused inside of motor to fill with grease.

Investigate Why

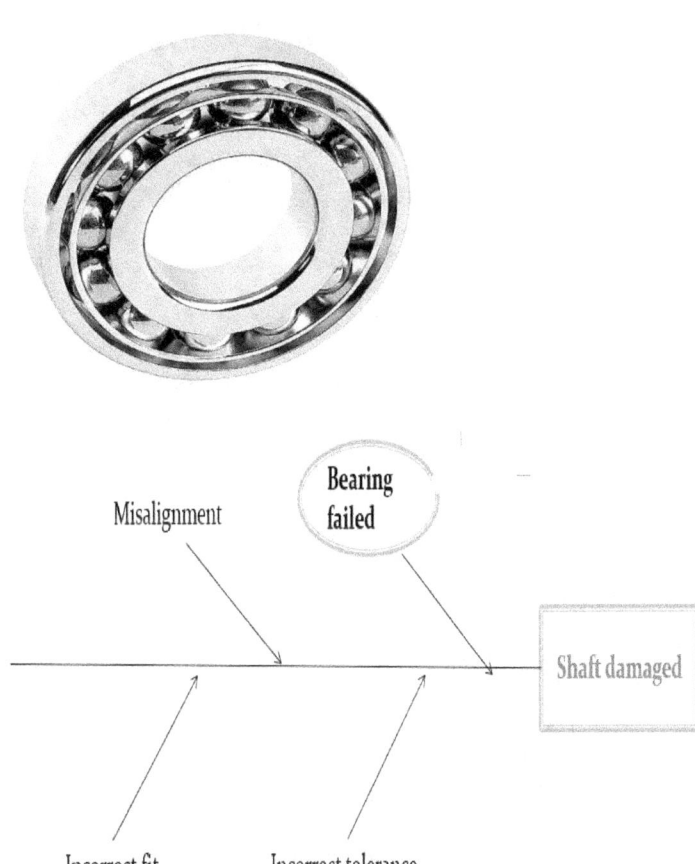

Investigate Why

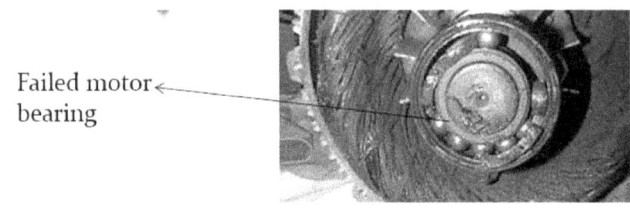

Failed motor bearing

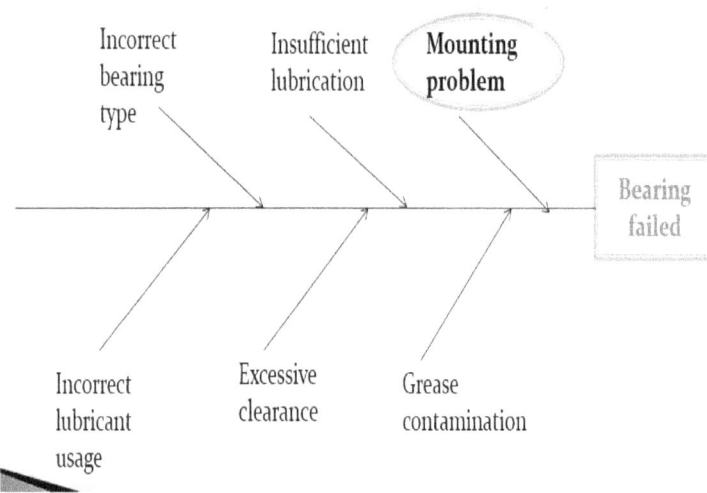

Incorrect bearing type

Insufficient lubrication

Mounting problem

Bearing failed

Incorrect lubricant usage

Excessive clearance

Grease contamination

Preventive Action

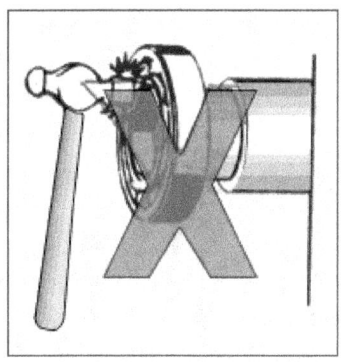

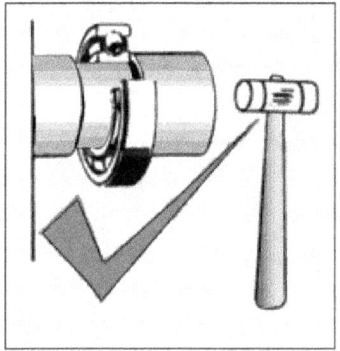

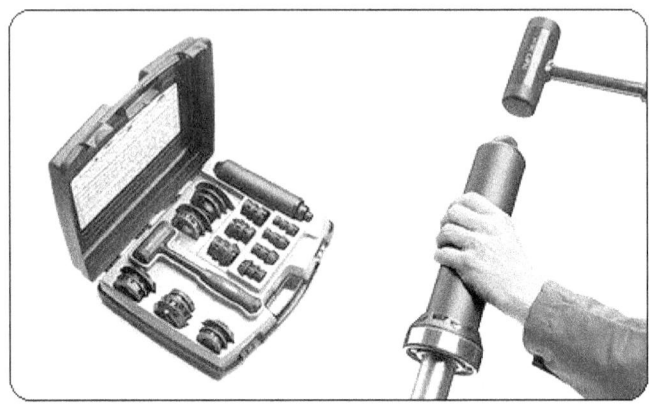

Use the proper tools for mounting and
train the maintenance crew

About the Author

 Mohammed Hamed Ahmed Soliman is an industrial engineer, consultant, university lecturer, operational excellence leader, and author. He works as a lecturer at the American University in Cairo and as a consultant for several international industrial organizations.

Soliman earned a bachelor of science in Engineering and a master's degree in Quality Management. He earned post-graduate degrees in Industrial Engineering and Engineering Management. He holds numerous certificates in management, industry, quality, and cost engineering.

For most of his career, Soliman worked as a regular employee for various industrial sectors. This included crystal-glass making, fertilizers, and chemicals. He did this while educating people about the culture of continuous improvement.

Soliman has lectured at Princess Noura

University and trained the maintenance team in Vale Oman Pelletizing Company. He has been lecturing at The American University in Cairo for 6 year and has designed and delivered 40 leadership and technical skills enhancement training modules.

Soliman is a member at the Institute of Industrial and Systems Engineers and a member with the Society for Engineering and Management Systems. He has published several articles in peer reviewed academic journals and magazines. His writings on lean manufacturing, leadership, productivity, and business appear in Industrial Engineers, Lean Thinking, and Industrial Management. Soliman's blog is www.personal-lean.org.

References

Liker, J. K. (2003). Toyota way: 14 Management Principles. New York: MacGraw-hill.

Robert T. Amsden and Davida M. Amsdenand. (1998). SPC Simplified: Practical steps to quality. Productivity Press; 2 editions.

Steven, S. (2012). Strategic lean mapping. New York: MacGraw-hill.

Rick Harris, Chris Harris, Earl Wilson, Jim Womack, Dan Jones, John Shook, Jose Ferro. 2003. Making Materials Flow: A Lean Material-Handling Guide for Operations, Production-Control, and Engineering Professionals; version 1.0 Edition.

Liker, J.K. 2002. The Toyota Way: 14 Management Principles from the World's Greatest Manufacturer.

Liker, J. K., and D. Meier. 2005. The Toyota
Way Fieldbook: A Practical Guide for
Implementing Toyota's 4Ps. New York:
McGraw-Hill.

Rother, M. 2009. The Toyota Kata:
Managing People for Improvement,
Adaptiveness and Superior Results. New
York: McGraw-Hill.

Womack, J. P., and Jones, D.T. (1996). Lean
Thinking: Banish Waste and Create Wealth
in Your Corporation. Free Press.

Rother, M., Harris, R. 2001. Creating
Continuous Flow: Creating Continuous
Flow: An Action Guide for Managers,
Engineers & Production Associates. Lean
Enterprise Institute Publications.

Liker, J.K. The Toyota Way: 14
Management Principles from the World's
Greatest Manufacturer. McGraw-Hill
Educations.

Byrne, A. 2012. Lean Turnaround: The Lean
Turnaround: How Business Leaders Use

Lean Principles to Create Value and Transform Their Company. McGraw-Hill Educations.

Ahmed, M. H. (2013). Lean transformation guidance: Why organizations fail to achieve and sustain excellence through lean improvement. International Journal of Lean Thinking, 4(1), 31–40.

Ahmed, M. H. (2014). Daily walks train future leaders. Industrial Management, 56(1), 22–27.

Soliman, M. H. A. (2015b). What Toyota production system is really about? (Unpublished). https://www.researchgate.net/publication/280557330_What_Toyota_Production_System_is_Really_About.

Soliman, M. H. A. (2015). A new routine for culture change. Industrial Management, 57(3), 25–30.

Soliman, M., A Comprehensive Review of
Manufacturing Wastes: Toyota Production
System Lean Principles, 2017.

Soliman, M. H. A. (2020). Takt Time, Cycle
Time, One-Piece Flow, and Heijunka.

Soliman, M. H. A. (2020). Kanban the
Toyota Way: An Inventory Buffering
System to Eliminate Inventory. KDP.

Soliman, M. H. A. (2017). Why continuous
improvement programs fail in the Egyptian
manufacturing organizations: A research
study of the evidence. American Journal of
Industrial and Business Management, 7(3),
202–222.
https://doi.org/10.4236/ajibm.2017.73016

Soliman, M. H. A. (2016). Hoshin Kanri:
How Toyota creates a culture of continuous
improvement to achieve lean goals.
CreateSpace.

Soliman, M. H. A. (2020). Gemba Walks the
Toyota Way: The Place to Teach and Learn
Management. KDP.

Soliman, M. H. A. (2020). Jidoka - The Missing Pillar!

Soliman, M. H. A. (2020). Jidoka: The Toyota Principle of Building Quality into the Process. KDP.

More by Mohammed Hamed Ahmed Soliman